# Why VBA for Excel 2021 and Excel 365?

This book is about VBA for Microsoft Excel 2021 and VBA for Microsoft Excel 365. The installed versions only differ in the way of licensing. Only online version don't have VBA.

# How to use this book?

The chapters are sorted alphabetically for easy searching. Each chapter has three parts:
- **Result**
- **Solution**
- **Program code** (if you need it).

| | |
|---|---|
|  | Additional information is provided to the right of the arrow. |

The appendixes contain data enabling the extension of programs with options.

I wish you much satisfaction in putting my advice into practice.

*Klemens Nguyen*

# 1st step – Developer tab

The **Developer** tab is invisible (default). 1st step is make it visible.

---

## Result

---

## Solution

Follow the numbers.

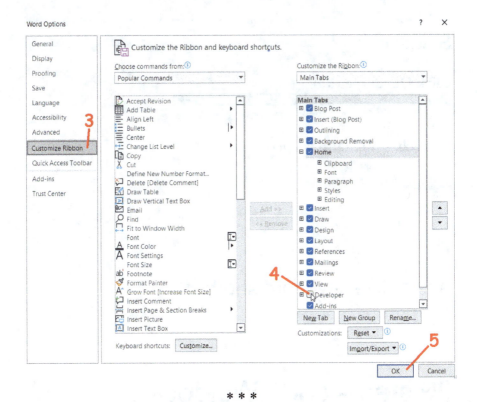

* * *

# 2nd step – VBA window

There are all tools in VBA Window.

# Result

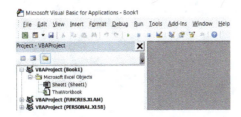

## Solution

Click **Developer** tab.

Then click **Visual Basic** icon.

Record Macro
Use Relative References
Macro Security

Visual Basic  Macros

Code

## Alternative keyboard shortcut

Alt+F11

\* \* \*

# 3rd step – code Window

Code Window is place when you can write VBA program. Here you see macro code.

## Result

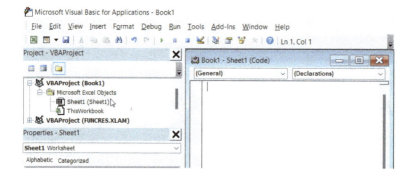

## Solution

1. Simply double click here.

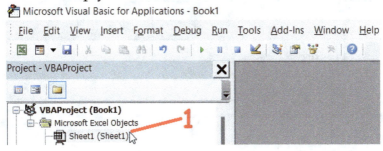

## Keyboard shortcut

F7

* * *

# Addressing cells (A1, B3, etc.)

See the chapter „**Cell as a variable**".

# Addressing cells by row and column number

In example the program reads the data from cells (1,1) and (2,1), sum them up, and save the result in cell (3,1).

# Result

| | A |
|---|---|
| 1 | 7 |
| 2 | 9 |
| 3 | |

before

| | A |
|---|---|
| 1 | 7 |
| 2 | 9 |
| 3 | 63 |

after

---

# Screenshot

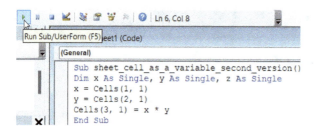

---

# Program code

```
Sub sheet_cell_as_a_variable_second_version()
Dim x As Single, y As Single, z As Single
x = Cells(1, 1)
y = Cells(2, 1)
Cells(3, 1) = x * y
End Sub
```

* * *

# Assignment statement

## Result

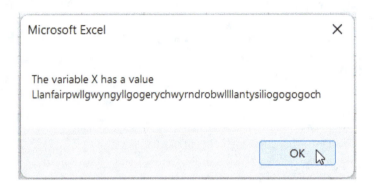

## Screenshot

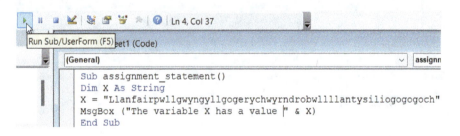

## Program code

```
Sub assignment_statement()
Dim X As String
```

X = "Llanfairpwllgwyngyllgogerychwyrndrobwllllantysiliogogog och"

MsgBox ("The variable X has a value " & X)

End Sub

|  | Llanfairpwllgwyngyllgogerychwyrndrobwllllanty-siliogogogoch is a large village in North West Wales, Europe. |
|---|---|

\* \* \*

# Batch file

## Result

This is Windows Batch File.

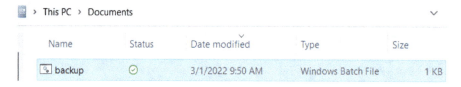

## Screenshot

Follow the numbers.

1 – Write code in Notepad.

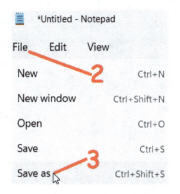

2 – Click **File**.

3 – Click **Save as**.

4- Choose file location.

5 – Format.

6 – File name.

7 – Click **Save**.

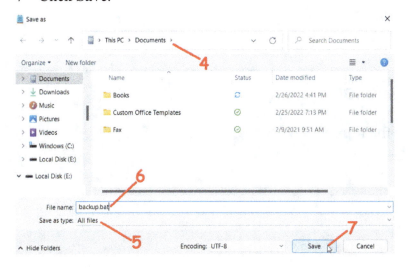

---

# Program code

copy E:\backup1\*.docx E:\backup2\

\* \* \*

---

# Button

In VBA you can place own button.

---

## Result

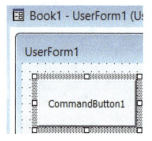

---

## Screenshot

Follow the numbers.

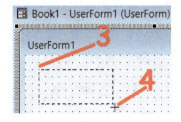

Drag from point „3" to point „4".

.

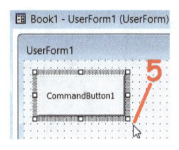

Default buttons's name is CommandButton1.

\* \* \*

# Button – aligning

## Result

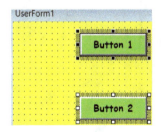

## Screenshot

Follow the numbers.

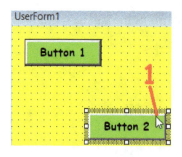

1 - Select the reference button

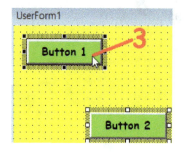

2- Press and hold **Shift.**

3 – Click next button.

4 - Release **Shift.**

5 – Select how the buttons are aligned (for example Lefts).

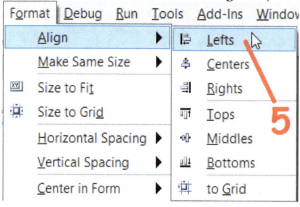

\* \* \*

# Button – back color

## Result

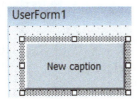

## Screenshot

Follow the numbers.

1. Click black arrow.

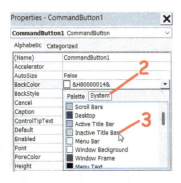

2. Click **System**.

3. Choose color.

\* \* \*

# Button – back color (second option)

## Result

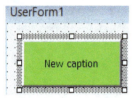

## Screenshot

Follow the numbers.

There is more collors in **Palette** than in System.

\* \* \*

# Button – caption

## Result

The caption (text on button) can be edited.

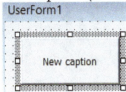

## Screenshot

Follow the numbers.

1.  Click here.

2.  Delete default name.

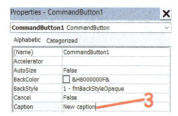

3. Write own name.

* * *

# Button – center

## Result

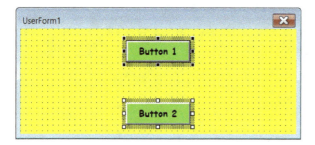

## Screenshot

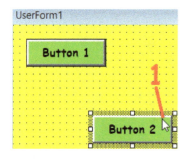

1. Click button.
2. Press and hold **Shift**.

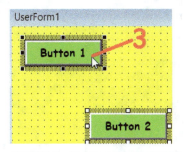

3. Click another button

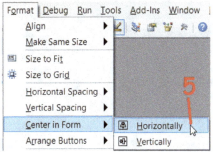

4. Release **Shift**.
5. Select how the buttons are centered (for example Horizontally).

\* \* \*

# Button – font

## Result

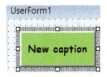

## Screenshot

Follow the numbers.

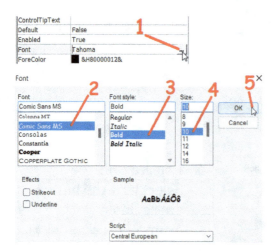

# Button – height

## Result

## Screenshot

Follow the numbers.

1. Click button.

2. Click here.

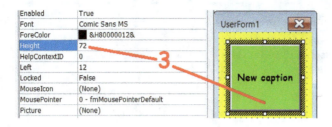

3. Write new button's height.

* * *

# Button – returned values

Which button was pressed? The information is contained in the variable.

___

## Result

What does the value of the variable x mean? Value of variable depends on button

___

## Solution

**Run** program. The first window displays buttons. The second window displays the value of the variable.

___

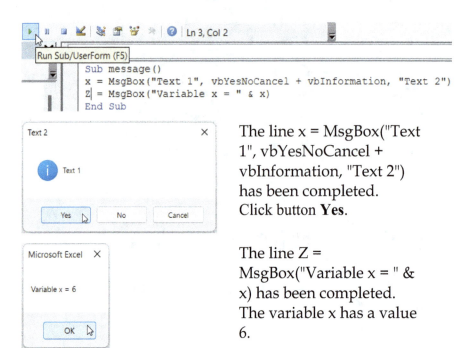

The line x = MsgBox("Text 1", vbYesNoCancel + vbInformation, "Text 2") has been completed. Click button **Yes**.

The line Z = MsgBox("Variable x = " & x) has been completed. The variable x has a value 6.

| | |
|---|---|
|  | More options of MsgBox – see Appendix A. |
|  | More return values – see Table 1. |

Table 1. Return values

| Button | Value |
|--------|-------|
| OK | 1 |
| Cancel | 2 |
| Abort | 3 |
| Retry | 4 |
| Ignore | 5 |
| Yes | 6 |
| No | 7 |

See Table 1, row with word **Yes**. In this same row in column there is number **6** – like on pictures above.

| | |
|---|---|
|  | Pressing the **Esc** key has the same effect as clicking the **Cancel** button. |

## Program code

```
Sub message()
x = MsgBox("Text 1", vbYesNoCancel + vbInformation,
"Text 2")
Z = MsgBox("Variable x = " & x)
End Sub
```

\* \* \*

# Buttons one by one

## Result

## Screenshot

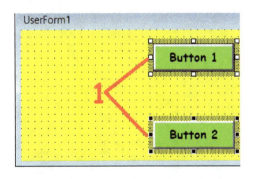

1. Select buttons.

---

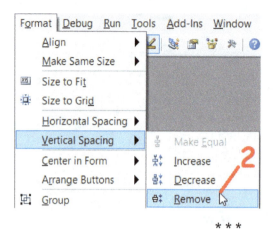

2. Choose: **Format**, **Vertical Spacing**, **Remove**.

\* \* \*

# Buttons the same size

---

# Result

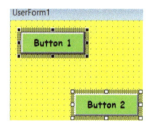

## Screenshot

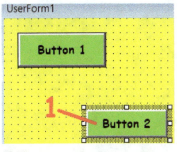

1 – Click button.

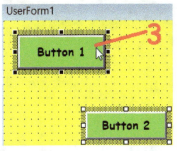

2 – Press and hold **Shift**.

3 – Click next button.

4 - Release **Shift.**

5 – Click **Both**.

\* \* \*

# Cell as a variable

The program reads the data from cells A1 and A2, sum them up, and save the result in cell A3.

# Result

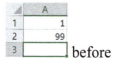

before

after

# Screenshot

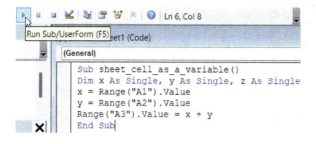

# Program code

```
Sub sheet_cell_as_a_variable()
Dim x As Single, y As Single, z As Single
x = Range("A1").Value
y = Range("A2").Value
Range("A3").Value = x + y
End Sub
```

* * *

# Copying the first N characters from cell A1 into cell B1

## Results

## Screenshot

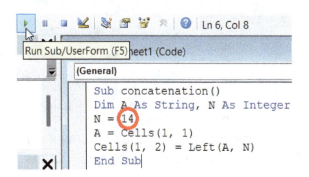

Program copy the first N=14 characters from cell A1 into cell B1.

## Program code

```
Sub concatenation()
Dim A As String, N As Integer
N = 14
A = Cells(1, 1)
Cells(1, 2) = Left(A, N)
End Sub
```

\* \* \*

# Current date – cell

The value of a variable can be written to a cell.

## Result

Cell A1 – text. Cell A2 - value of a variable

| | A | B | C |
|---|---|---|---|
| 1 | The variable t has the value: | 3/16/2022 | |

B1    fx   3/16/2022

## Solution

Run the program (below). Second line means: variable t= system date. On the next line, text The variable t has the value: is entered into cell A1. Fifth row: the value of the variable t is stored in cell B1.

Run Sub/UserForm (F5)    Ln 5, Col 8

```
Sub Current_Date ()
t = Date$
Cells(1, 1) = "The variable t has the value: "
Cells(1, 2) = t
End Sub
```

Look at the Excel sheet (below).

The cells are too narrow. Drag the lines separating the cells (see - Result).

## Program code

```
Sub Current_Date()
t = Date$
Cells(1, 1) = "The variable t has the value: "
Cells(1, 2) = t
End Sub
```

* * *

# Current date – variable

## Result

The variable t has the value Date$. Date as a variable value

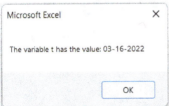

## Solution

**Date $** reads the date. So the variable t = system date. The next line displays the text *The variable t has the value:* and the value of the variable **t** (picture 21).

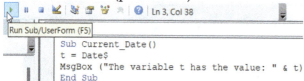

```
Sub Current_Date()
t = Date$
MsgBox ("The variable t has the value: " & t)
End Sub
```

On picture above A variable t. Value assignment and display.

## Program code

```
Sub Current_Date()
t = Date$
MsgBox ("The variable t has the value: " & t)
End Sub
```

* * *

# Current date form mm/dd/yyyy

## Result

VBA can read the current system date.

---

# Solution

Run program (picture below).

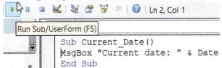

```
Sub Current_Date()
MsgBox "Current date: " & Date
End Sub
```

Look at the Excel sheet (see Result).

---

# Program code

Sub Current_Date()
MsgBox "Current date: " & Date
End Sub

* * *

---

# Current date form mm-dd-yyyy

## Result

VBA can read the current system date (below).

There is the current system date *mm-dd-yyyy* in the picture

## Solution

Run program (below).

Program for displaying the system date in form *mm-dd-yyyy*.
Look at the Excel sheet (see Result).

## Program code

Sub Current_Date()
MsgBox "Current date: " & Date$
End Sub

                                     \* \* \*

# Date – default value

---

## Result

The default value is different from the system date. It is not the same.

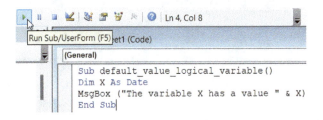

---

## Screenshot

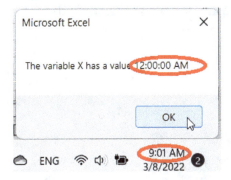

```
Sub default_value_logical_variable()
Dim X As Date
MsgBox ("The variable X has a value " & X)
End Sub
```

---

## Program code

Sub default_value_logical_variable()
Dim X As Date

---

MsgBox ("The variable X has a value " & X)
End Sub

\* \* \*

# Deleting a macro loaded with a sheet

If the macro was saved in **Personal Macro Workbook** then it will be run every time Excel is started.

## Results

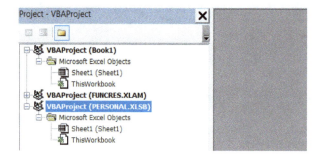

## Solution

Right-click **Module**.
Choose **Remove Module**.

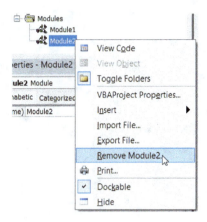

Click **No**.

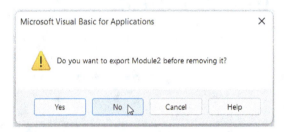

Repeat the above steps until all modules are removed.

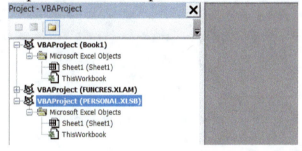

Right-click the icon on the **Quick Access Toolbar**.

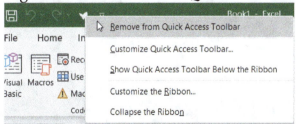

Click on the cross in the upper right corner of the sheet.

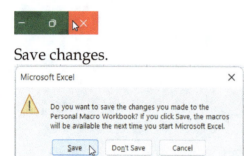

Save changes.

* * *

# Dialog box with OK button

---

## Result

---

## Screenshot

```
Book1 - Sheet1 (Code)
(General)                              Raport
    Sub Raport()
    x = MsgBox("Message", vbOKOnly + vbInformation, "Title")
    End Sub
```

## Program code

```
Sub Raport()
x = MsgBox("Message", vbOKOnly + vbInformation, "Title")
End Sub
```

\* \* \*

# Different types of the same variable in separate procedures

## Result

          and                    is true

# Screenshot

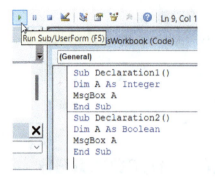

Run program.

Choose subroutine with number **1**. Click **Run**.

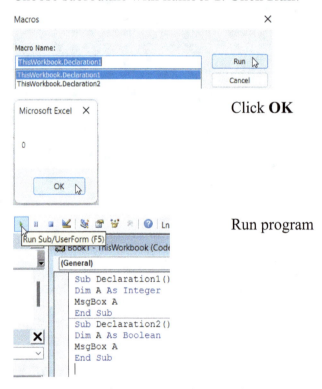

Click **OK**

Run program

Choose subroutine with number **2**. Click **Run**.

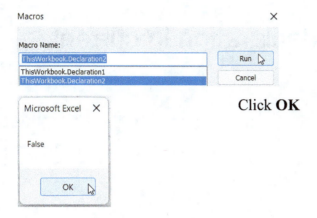

Click **OK**

# Program code

Sub Declaration1()
Dim A As Integer
MsgBox A
End Sub
Sub Declaration2()
Dim A As Boolean
MsgBox A
End Sub

 The same variable in different procedures can store different data types.

\* \* \*

# Duplicate declaration in current scope

## Result

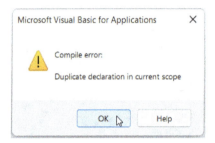

## Screenshot

One variable, but two types (below).

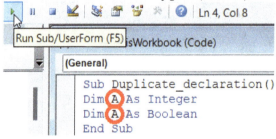

## Program code

Sub Duplicate_declaration()

```
Dim A As Integer
Dim A As Boolean
End Sub
```

\* \* \*

# Entering characters that aren't on the keyboard

There are most commonly used characters on the keyboard. How to enter other, like: μ, © or €?

---

## Result

Where is the μ symbol on the keyboard?

---

## Solution

Launch the program (below). The variable i = 181. Function Chr(i) returns a string containing the character associated with the specified character code.

---

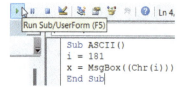

```
Sub ASCII()
i = 181
x = MsgBox((Chr(i)))
End Sub
```

Look at the Excel sheet (Result).

---

## Program code

```
Sub ASCII()
i = 181
x = MsgBox((Chr(i)))
End Sub
```

 See Appendix B for codes for other characters.

* * *

# Entering data

---

## Results

# Screenshot

|  | The position of the insertion point (cursor) on pressing **F5** indicates the procedure that will be run. |

Run the program.

## Click **main** and then **Run**.

## Enter data.

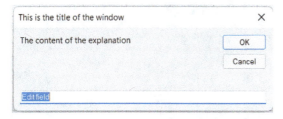

## Clik **OK**.

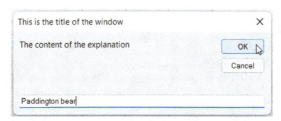

## Program code

```
Option Explicit
Dim A As String
Dim B As String
Sub main()
reader
writer
End Sub
Sub reader()
A = InputBox("The content of the explanation", "This is the
title of the window", "Edit field")
End Sub
Sub writer()
B = MsgBox("In the edit field you entered: " & A)
End Sub
```

\* \* \*

# Writing data to the cell

## Results

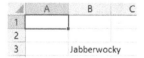

## Screenshot

Run program.

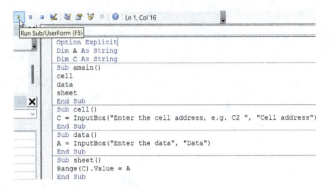

```
Option Explicit
Dim A As String
Dim C As String
Sub amain()
cell
data
sheet
End Sub
Sub cell()
C = InputBox("Enter the cell address, e.g. C2 ", "Cell address")
End Sub
Sub data()
A = InputBox("Enter the data", "Data")
End Sub
Sub sheet()
Range(C).Value = A
End Sub
```

Click **amain** and **Run**.

Ennet cell name. Click **OK**.

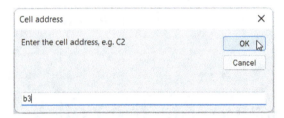

Eneter data. Click **OK**.

See Result.

## Program code

```
Option Explicit
Dim A As String
Dim C As String
Sub amain()
cell
data
sheet
End Sub
Sub cell()
C = InputBox("Enter the cell address, e.g. C2 ", "Cell address")
End Sub
Sub data()
A = InputBox("Enter the data", "Data")
End Sub
Sub sheet()
Range(C).Value = A
End Sub
```

* * *

# Entering the value into the cell

## Result

| A2 | | ⅄ | ✓ | *fx* | 3.1415926 |
|----|---|---|---|------|-----------|
| | A | B | C | D | |
| 1 | | | | | |
| 2 | 3.1415926 | | | | |

## Screenshot

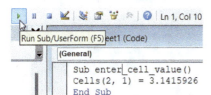

There is number 102 in cell **A2**.

**Run** the program. See result (in Result of course)

## Program code

Sub enter_cell_value()
Cells(2, 1) = 3.1415926
End Sub

* * *

# Files management commands

- **del** – deleting files and directories,
- **copy** – copying files and directories,
- **rename** – renaming files or folders,
- **dir** – display the contents of a folder,
- **cmd** – launching the command prompt,
- **md** – creating a directory,
- **chdir** – displays the name of or changes the current directory,
- **exit** – closing the command prompt,
- **command_name /?** – information about command.

* * *

# Local variables

## Result

The procedure **Declaration1** displays default value of variable A.

The procedure **Declaration2** displays default value of variable A.

The procedure **Declarations** runs procedure **Declaration1**, assigns the variable A = 1. The next line displays the window with information about the value of variable A.
In the second procedure, the variable defaults to zero. The next line displays a window with information about the value of variable A.

|  | The procedure is invoked by giving its name |
|---|---|

# Screenshot

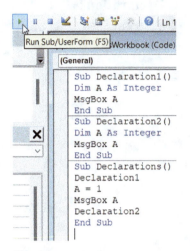

**Run** program.

```
Sub Declaration1()
Dim A As Integer
MsgBox A
End Sub
Sub Declaration2()
Dim A As Integer
MsgBox A
End Sub
Sub Declarations()
Declaration1
A = 1
MsgBox A
Declaration2
End Sub
```

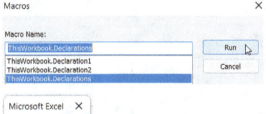

Click **Declarations** and **Run**.

Default value of variable is **0**. It was subroutine **Declaration1**.

Variable **A** after **A=1**.

Default value of variable is **0**. It was subroutine **Declaration2**.

## Program code

```
Sub Declaration1()
Dim A As Integer
MsgBox A
End Sub
Sub Declaration2()
Dim A As Integer
MsgBox A
End Sub
Sub Declarations()
Declaration1
A = 1
MsgBox A
Declaration2
End Sub
```

* * *

# Logical variable – default value

## Result

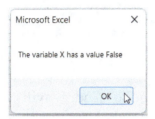

## Screenshot

Simply – run program.

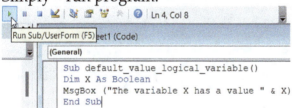

## Program code

```
Sub default_value_logical_variable()
Dim X As Boolean
MsgBox ("The variable X has a value " & X)
End Sub
```

* * *

# Loop – checking the condition

The program will display a window asking you to enter the string. If nothing is entered, he will ask for it again. After entering the string, the program will display it in the message window and exit.

## Result

As long as the variable has nothing assigned, a window will appear asking you to enter the string (below).

## Solution

The program consists of two subroutines: **non_empty** and **message**.

A **non_empty** subroutine begins by clearing a string variable. It is not necessary when the first time you start the program. If the program is executed again, the string variable is assigned the value ... from the previous execution. The statements between **Do Until** and **Loop** are executed until the condition <> "" is true. If the condition is true, it means that the string variable **data** is not empty.

As long as the variable has nothing assigned, a window will appear asking you to enter the string. When you type a string, it is assigned to the variable **data**. The **message** procedure will then be executed to display the contents of the variable **data**. **Run** program (below).

Next window depends on where the insertion mark is (in red).

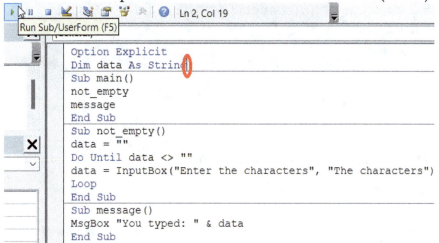

Select **Sheet1.main** and click **Run**.

data = InputBox("Enter the characters", "The characters") - done Click **OK**.

There is window as in picture above. Write some sings and click **OK** (below). In example string is „Paddington bear".

Sub **message** done (result below – it is value of variable data). Click **OK**.

The program has ended. Again the window **Code** (below).

```
(General)
Option Explicit
Dim data As String
Sub main()
not_empty
message
End Sub
Sub not_empty()
data = ""
Do Until data <> ""
data = InputBox("Enter the characters", "The characters")
Loop
End Sub
Sub message()
MsgBox "You typed: " & data
End Sub
```

# Program code

Option Explicit
Dim data As String
Sub main()
not_empty
message
End Sub
Sub not_empty()
data = ""

```
Do Until data <> ""
data = InputBox("Enter the characters", "The characters")
Loop
End Sub
Sub message()
MsgBox "You typed: " & data
End Sub
```

---

## Exercise

In the window enter a space instead of the string.

\* \* \*

# Loop – non-empty condition

What to do when this number of loop repetitions unknown and e.g. the program is to run until it finds an empty cell?

---

## Result

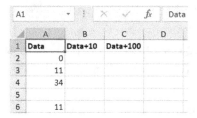

In picture on the left - the test data

| A1 | ▼ | ⋮ | ✕ | ✓ | *fx* | Data | |
|---|---|---|---|---|---|---|---|

| ▲ | A | B | C | D |
|---|---|---|---|---|
| 1 | Data | Data+10 | Data+100 | |
| 2 | 0 | 10 | 100 | |
| 3 | 11 | 21 | 111 | |
| 4 | 34 | 44 | 134 | |
| 5 | | | | |
| 6 | 11 | | | |

In this picture - the sheet after executing the program i.e. results od addition

## Solutions

Launch the program (picture 35).
Option **Explicit means** that you must explicitly declare all variables.
There is a subroutine between **Sub** and **End Sub**.
**Non_empty()** it is name of the subroutine.
**Dim i As Integer** - this is a declaration for the variable i. It can only take integer values.
The columns have headers (picture 33). Therefore, the addition starts at line 2. At the beginning **i = 2**.

There is loop between **Do While** and **Loop**. The statements after **Do While** will be executed when the condition **Cells(i, 1).Value <> ""** is true.
**Cells(i, 1).Value** means a contents of the cell with the address (i, 1).
The condition **<> ""** is true when the content of **cell (i, 1)** is less than or greater than the empty cell. It is false when **cell (i, 1)** is empty.
When the condition is true, the statement **Cells(i, 2).Value = Cells(i, 1).Value + 10** is executed. The data is read from the cell **Cells(i, 1)**, increased by 10 and stored in the cell **Cells(i, 2)**.
Then next statement is executed. The data is read from the cell **Cells(i, 1)**, increased by 100 and stored in the cell **Cells(i, 3)**.
The variable i is incremented by 1.
In other words the loop runs until data is read from an empty cell.

```
Option Explicit
Sub non_empty()
Dim i As Integer
i = 2
Do While Cells(i, 1).Value <> ""
    Cells(i, 2).Value = Cells(i, 1).Value + 10
    Cells(i, 3).Value = Cells(i, 1).Value + 100
    i = i + 1
Loop
End Sub
```

## Program code

```
Option Explicit
Sub non_empty()
Dim i As Integer
i = 2
Do While Cells(i, 1).Value <> ""
Cells(i, 2).Value = Cells(i, 1).Value + 10
Cells(i, 3).Value = Cells(i, 1).Value + 100
i = i + 1
Loop
End Sub
```

* * *

# Loop – step

The value of the variable does not have to change by 1. The step can have any value.

## Result

For example, this option allows you to enter text only into even cells.

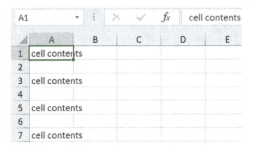

## Solution

Launch the program (below).

The code lines between For and Next will be repeated. For i = 1, subroutine enters the string **cell contents** into the cell at the intersection of row 1 and column 1. Next subroutine reaches **Next i**. It increases **i** with **2** and jumps back to the **For** statement. For **i = 3**, subroutine enters the string **cell contents** into the cell at the intersection of row 3 and column 1. Next subroutine reaches **Next i**. It increases **i** with **2** and jumps back to the **For** statement. For **i = 5**, subroutine enters the string **cell contents** into the cell at the intersection of row 5 and column 1, etc.

Below subroutine with step 2

```
Option Explicit
Sub step_two()
Dim i As Integer
    For i = 1 To 8 Step 2
        Cells(i, 1).Value = "cell contents"
    Next i
End Sub
```

## Program code

Option Explicit

```
Sub step_two()
Dim i As Integer
For i = 1 To 8 Step 2
Cells(i, 1).Value = "cell contents"
Next i
End Sub
```

* * *

# Loop with negative step

The loop step can be negative. The position of the cells can be any (below).

---

## Result

Subroutine enters the sing X form B2 to H2.

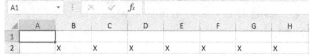

---

## Solution

Launch the program (picture 39).
**Dim i As Integer** - this is a declaration for the variable i. It can only take integer values. A loop is between **For i** and **Next i**. The initial value of the variable i is **8**. Each loop execution decreases **i** by **1**. Each time the loop is executed, **X** is written to the cell **(2, i)**. The command **Next i** returns to the **For** statement.
The program below inserts seven „X".

---

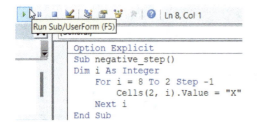

```
Option Explicit
Sub negative_step()
Dim i As Integer
    For i = 8 To 2 Step -1
        Cells(2, i).Value = "X"
    Next i
End Sub
```

# Program code

```
Option Explicit
Sub negative_step()
Dim i As Integer
For i = 8 To 2 Step -1
Cells(2, i).Value = "X"
Next i
End Sub
```

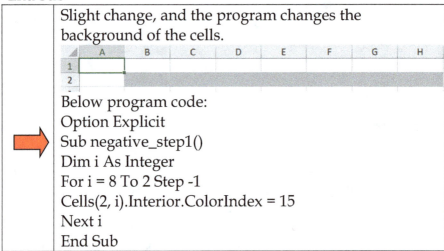

Slight change, and the program changes the background of the cells.

Below program code:
```
Option Explicit
Sub negative_step1()
Dim i As Integer
For i = 8 To 2 Step -1
Cells(2, i).Interior.ColorIndex = 15
Next i
End Sub
```

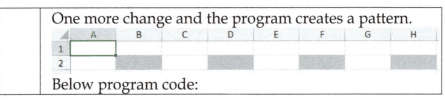

One more change and the program creates a pattern.

Below program code:

```
Option Explicit
Sub negative_step2()
Dim i As Integer
For i = 8 To 2 Step -2
Cells(2, i).Interior.ColorIndex = 15
Next i
End Sub
```

Chessboard? Here you are!

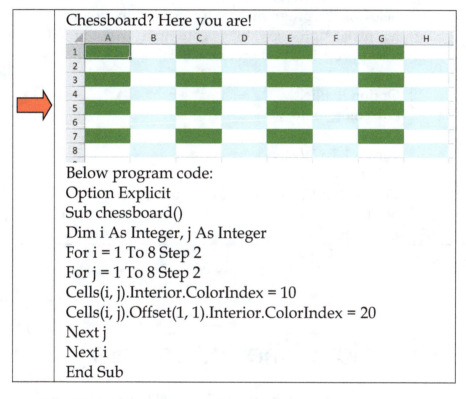

Below program code:

```
Option Explicit
Sub chessboard()
Dim i As Integer, j As Integer
For i = 1 To 8 Step 2
For j = 1 To 8 Step 2
Cells(i, j).Interior.ColorIndex = 10
Cells(i, j).Offset(1, 1).Interior.ColorIndex = 20
Next j
Next i
End Sub
```

What is the dependence between ColorIndex and cell color? Here is part of color template.

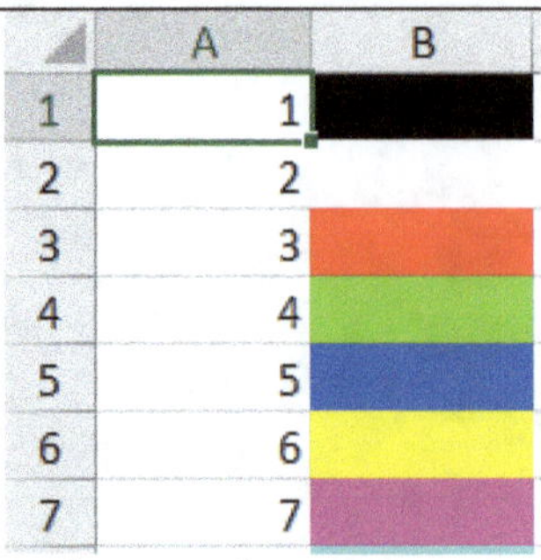

|   | A | B |
|---|---|---|
| 1 | 1 | |
| 2 | 2 | |
| 3 | 3 | |
| 4 | 4 | |
| 5 | 5 | |
| 6 | 6 | |
| 7 | 7 | |

Below is the program code for making the color template. Numeric value in column A. In column B - the appropriate background color:

```
Option Explicit
Sub color_template()
Dim i As Integer
For i = 1 To 56 Step 1
Cells(i, 1) = i
Cells(i, 2).Interior.ColorIndex = i
Next i
End Sub
```

* * *

# The color of the cell borders

VBA can easily change the color of the cell borders (picture below).

## Results

Red? Green? Blue or maybe pink? With just one click, you can change the color of the border lines across the sheet. It is power of VBA

| | A | B | C |
|---|---|---|---|
| 1 | | | |
| 2 | | | |
| 3 | | | |
| 4 | | | |
| 5 | | | |

## Solution

Run the program (picture XX). Dependence between ColorIndex and color you find in chapter Loop with negative step.

```
Sub Color_Cell_Borders()
    Cells.Borders.ColorIndex = 5
End Sub
```

## Program code

```
Sub Color_Cell_Borders()
Cells.Borders.ColorIndex = 5
End Sub
```

*  *  *

# Loop Do While

The **For Next** loop is not the only one. The code between **Do While** and **Loop** will be repeated when the condition after **Do While** is true.

|  | Computer science is a field where the same effect can be achieved in different ways |
|---|---|

---

## Result

| A1 | | | ✕ | ✓ | fx | 102 |
|---|---|---|---|---|---|---|

|   | A | B | C | D |
|---|---|---|---|---|
| 1 | 102 | | | |
| 2 | 102 | | | |
| 3 | 102 | | | |
| 4 | 102 | | | |
| 5 | 102 | | | |
| 6 | 102 | | | |
| 7 | 102 | | | |

---

## Solution

Launch the program (picture 32).
Option **Explicit means** that you must explicitly declare all variables.
There is a subroutine between **Sub** and **End Sub**.
**Loop4()** it is name of the subroutine. **Dim i As Integer** - this is a declaration for the variable i. It can only take integer values.
Then the variable **i** is assigned the value **1**.
There is a loop between **Do While** and **Loop**.
As long as **i** is lower than 8, subroutine enters the value 102 into the cell at the intersection of row **i** and column 1 and increments **i** by **1**.

In other words the value 102 will be placed into column A seven times. Subroutine The subroutine will be executed the last time at i = 7. Then the condition i <8 will be fulfilled.

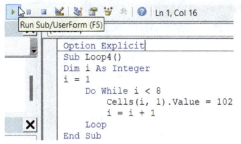

## Program code

```
Option Explicit
Sub Loop4()
Dim i As Integer
i = 1
Do While i < 8
Cells(i, 1).Value = 102
i = i + 1
Loop
End Sub
```

 In programming languages the symbol **=** means „becomes". So i = i + 1 means **i becomes i + 1**. So if i = 1, **i** becomes 1 + 1 = 2.

* * *

# Loop Double

A double loop allows you to operate on a two-dimensional range of cells.

# Result

A double loop fills a two-dimensional range of cells (see below). . Changed: row number and column number.

| A1 | | | ✕ | ✓ | fx | 99 |
|---|---|---|---|---|---|---|

| | A | B | C | D |
|---|---|---|---|---|
| 1 | 99 | 99 | | |
| 2 | 99 | 99 | | |
| 3 | 99 | 99 | | |
| 4 | 99 | 99 | | |
| 5 | 99 | 99 | | |
| 6 | 99 | 99 | | |
| 7 | 99 | 99 | | |

# Solution

Launch the program (picture 28).
For variables $i = 1$ and $j = 1$, subroutine writes the value 99 into the cell at the intersection of row 1 and column 1. When subroutine reaches **Next j**, it increases variable $j$ with 1 and jumps back to the **For j** statement. For $i = 1$ and $j = 2$, subroutine writes the value 99 into the cell at the intersection of row 1 and column 2. Next, subroutine ignores **Next j** because $j$ only runs from 1 to 2. When subroutine reaches **Next i**, it increases $i$ with 1 and jumps back to the **For i** statement. For variables $i = 2$ and $j = 1$, subroutine enters the value 99 into the cell at the intersection of row 2 and column 1, etc.
In other words when the loop is in a loop, the program is easier to read when the start and end of the same loop are offset from the left margin by the same number of Tab presses.

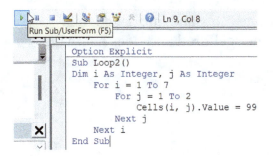

```
Run Sub/UserForm (F5)

Option Explicit
Sub Loop2()
Dim i As Integer, j As Integer
    For i = 1 To 7
        For j = 1 To 2
            Cells(i, j).Value = 99
        Next j
    Next i
End Sub
```

## Program code

```
Option Explicit
Sub Loop2()
Dim i As Integer, j As Integer
For i = 1 To 7
For j = 1 To 2
Cells(i, j).Value = 99
Next j
Next i
End Sub
```

\* \* \*

# Loop Single

A single loop allows you to operate on a one-dimensional range of cells.

## Result

A single loop fills a one-dimensional range of cells (see below).

In other words - seven or one thousand and seven cells - it doesn't matter. VBA does not get tired and does not make mistakes.

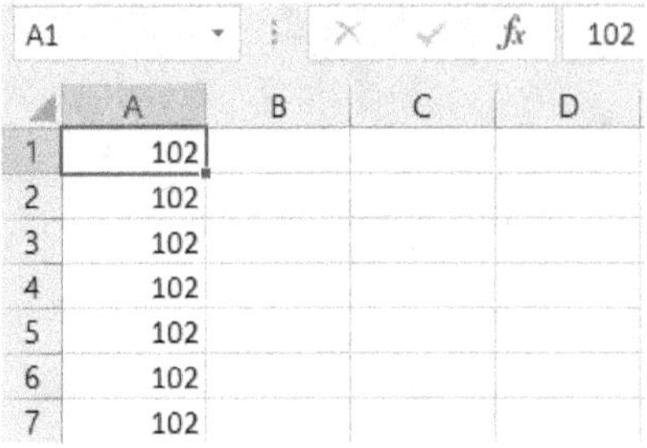

| | A | B | C | D |
|---|---|---|---|---|
| 1 | 102 | | | |
| 2 | 102 | | | |
| 3 | 102 | | | |
| 4 | 102 | | | |
| 5 | 102 | | | |
| 6 | 102 | | | |
| 7 | 102 | | | |

A1      fx   102

# Solution

Launch the program (picture below).
Option **Explicit means** that you must explicitly declare all variables.
There is a subroutine between **Sub** and **End Sub**.
**Loop1()** it is name of the subroutine.
**Dim i As Integer** - this is a declaration for the variable i. It can only take integer values.
There is a loop between **For** and **Next**.
**For i = 1 To 7** means that the variable i takes values from 1 to 7 inclusive.
**Cells(i, 1).Value** is the command to assign an Excel cell with address (i, 1) a value. When executing the loop, **i** takes values from 1 to 7. Successive cells have addresses (1, 1), (2, 1), (3, 1) up to (7, 1).
In the range (1,1) to (7, 1) cells have the value **102**.
**Next i** that's the end of the loop. It's also a command to add 1 to i.
Below one-dimensional loop.

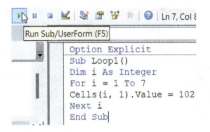

```
Option Explicit
Sub Loop1()
Dim i As Integer
For i = 1 To 7
Cells(i, 1).Value = 102
Next i
End Sub
```

## Program code

```
Option Explicit
Sub Loop1()
Dim i As Integer
For i = 1 To 7
Cells(i, 1).Value = 102
Next i
End Sub
```

 When in the program from Figure 26, instead of the line **Cells(i, 1).Value = 102**
you insert **Cells(i, 1).Value = i** cells from (1, 1) to (7, 1) will be filled with numbers from 1 to 7.

\* \* \*

# Loop Triple

A triple loop allows you to operate on a three-dimensional range of cells. What does it mean? The Excel sheet is two-dimensional. The third dimension could be a sheet number, for example.

 By default, Excel 2021 opens one sheet. To use multiple sheets, you need to create them.

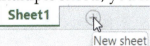

# Result

In this example, data has been entered into three sheets (there is the third dimension is the sheet number in the picture below).

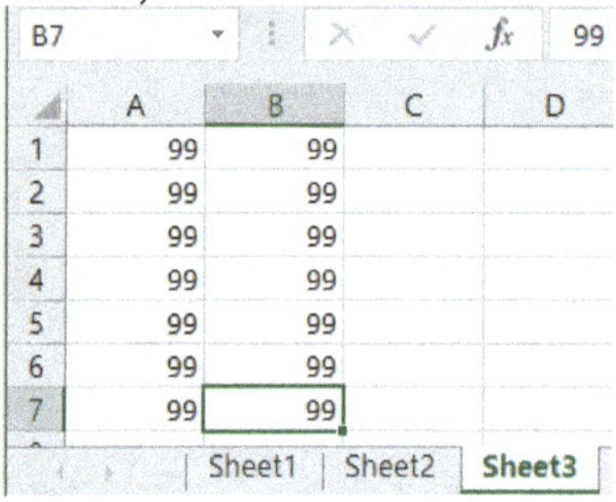

| | A | B | C | D |
|---|---|---|---|---|
| 1 | 99 | 99 | | |
| 2 | 99 | 99 | | |
| 3 | 99 | 99 | | |
| 4 | 99 | 99 | | |
| 5 | 99 | 99 | | |
| 6 | 99 | 99 | | |
| 7 | 99 | 99 | | |

B7    fx    99

Sheet1 | Sheet2 | **Sheet3**

# Solution

Launch the program (picture 30).
The program is similar to the previous example. Only the variable **s** and the **Worksheets (s)** command were added. The variable **s** takes the following values: 1, 2, and 3. Identical areas are filled in on **Sheet 1**, **Sheet 2** and **Sheet 3**.
In the picture there are three nested loops.

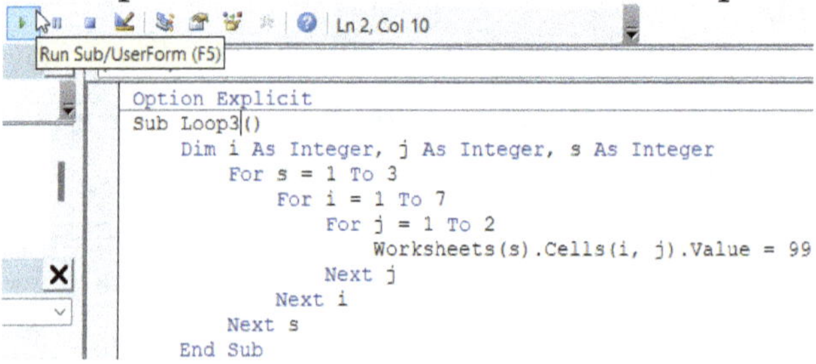

Ln 2, Col 10
Run Sub/UserForm (F5)

```
Option Explicit
Sub Loop3()
    Dim i As Integer, j As Integer, s As Integer
    For s = 1 To 3
        For i = 1 To 7
            For j = 1 To 2
                Worksheets(s).Cells(i, j).Value = 99
            Next j
        Next i
    Next s
End Sub
```

## Program code

```
Option Explicit
Sub Loop3()
Dim i As Integer, j As Integer, s As Integer
For s = 1 To 3
For i = 1 To 7
For j = 1 To 2
                    Worksheets(s).Cells(i, j).Value = 99
        Next j
        Next i
    Next s
    End Sub
```

* * *

# Macro on the toolbar

What does macro and VBA have in common? The macro is written in VBA.

## Result

Own program on the toolbar. It's very convenient.

## Solution

Step one - macro registration. Click the **Developer** tab. Click the **Record Macro** icon.

I named the macro **MyMacro**. If you select **Personal Macro Workbook**, the macro will be available in all workbooks.

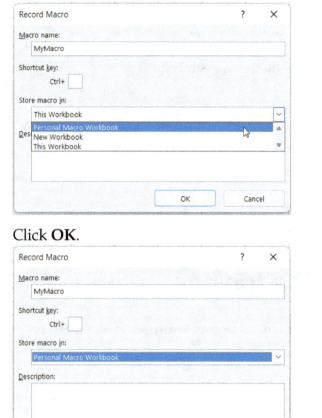

Click **OK**.

Click **Stop Recording**.

Open **VBA Editor**.

This macro does two things: places **Hello world!** In the active cell, and then selects cell **A2**.

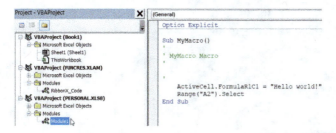

Click red cross in right upper corner of Visual Basic Editor.

Click the down arrow on the **Quick Access Toolbar** and click **More Commands**.

Under **Choose commands from**, select **Macros**. Select the macro. Click button **Add**.

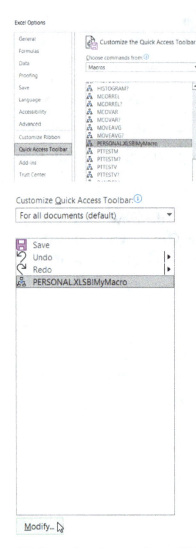

On the right side of the window, select the name of the program. Click the **Modify** button.

Click on the picture that will be shown on the button.

Click **OK**.

Click **OK** a second time.

There is a new button on the **Quick Access Toolbar**. Select **C1**. Click new **button**.

Text appears in the selected cell. As before, cell **A2** was selected.

Click on the cross in the upper right corner of the sheet.

To save the data, select the **Save** button.

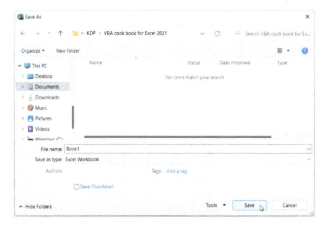

Please select a destination. Click the **Save** button.

If you want the macro to be available after running Excel on this computer, save it in **Personal Macro Workbook**.

It's time to check. Launch the **Excel**.

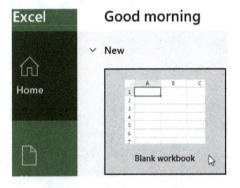

Choose **Blank Workbook**.

Our button is visible on the **Quick Access Toolbar**.

# Program code

Option Explicit
Sub MyMacro()
'

' MyMacro Macro

'

'

```
    ActiveCell.FormulaR1C1 = "Hello world!"
    Range("A2").Select
End Sub
```

* * *

# Mandatory declaration of variables

## Result

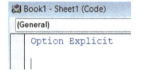

## Screenshot

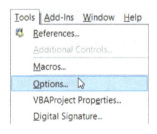

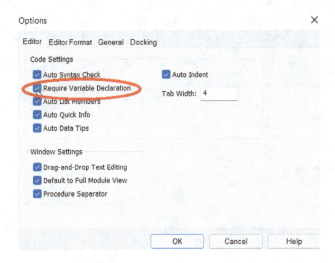

# Message box – many lines of text

A long message is difficult to read (below). How to split text into paragraphs?

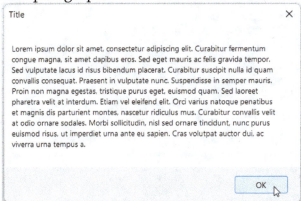

# Result

The programmer can use a linefeed character (below). This same text in four paragraphs.

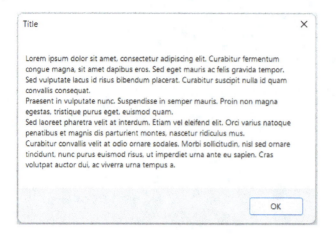

## Solution

Variables help organize the program. **Chr(10)** returns a linefeed character.

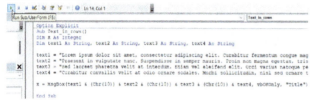

## Program code

I shortened the text. I put in "...".
Option Explicit
Sub Text_in_rows()
Dim x As Integer
Dim text1 As String, text2 As String, text3 As String, text4 As String

text1 = "Lorem ipsum… "

text2 = "Praesent in vulputate … "
text3 = "Sed laoreet…"
text4 = "Curabitur convallis..."

x = MsgBox(text1 & (Chr(10)) & text2 & (Chr(10)) & text3 &
(Chr(10)) & text4, vbOKOnly, "Title")
End Sub

\* \* \*

# Message box after button click

How to display the message window?

---

## Result

---

## Screenshot

Follow the numbers.

---

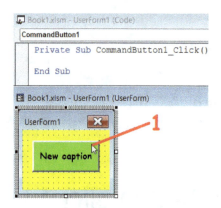

1    - Double click

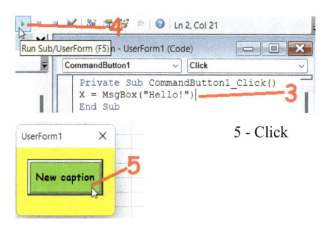

5 - Click

---

## Program code

```
Private Sub CommandButton1_Click()
X = MsgBox("Hello!")
End Sub
```

\* \* \*

# Opening file

How to open an Excel sheet from a program?

## Result

## Screenshot

## Program code

```
Sub Raport()
shell_1 = Shell("excel
C:\Users\wrote\Downloads\example.xlsx")
End Sub
```

\* \* \*

# Option explicit

What causes no variable declaration?

## Result

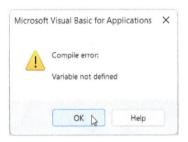

## Screenshot

Z - variable without declaration

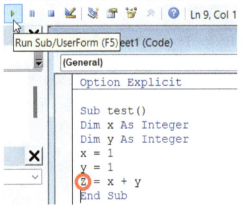

## Program code

Option Explicit
Sub test()
Dim x As Integer
Dim y As Integer
x = 1
y = 1
Z = x + y
End Sub

How to fix this error?
Solution below

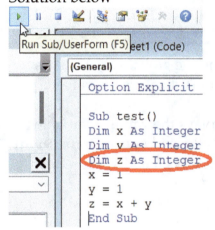

* * *

# Passing a value through a global variable

## Result

The program starts with declaring the global variable A as integer. The procedure **Declaration1** displays the value of variable A.
The procedure **Declaration2** displays the value of variable A. The procedure **Declarations** calls the procedure **Declaration1**. Then variable A is set to 1 and displays. Finally, procedure **Declaration2** will be displayed.

# Screenshots

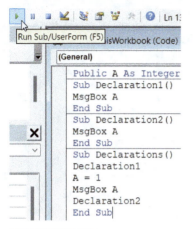

```
Public A As Integer
Sub Declaration1()
MsgBox A
End Sub
Sub Declaration2()
MsgBox A
End Sub
Sub Declarations()
Declaration1
A = 1
MsgBox A
Declaration2
End Sub
```

Sub Declaration1(). The variable has default value of 0.

Assign a value A=1 to a variable with global scope.

Sub Declaration2(). A=1 still

## Program code

```
Public A As Integer
Sub Declaration1()
MsgBox A
End Sub
Sub Declaration2()
MsgBox A
End Sub
Sub Declarations()
Declaration1
A = 1
MsgBox A
Declaration2
End Sub
```

* * *

# Path

Where is information about path?

## Result

## Screenshots

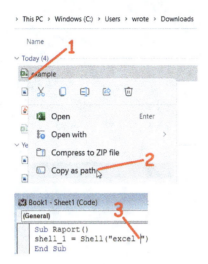

1 – right click file
2 – click
After that path is in
Clipboard.

3 – Ctrl+V and path is in
program

## Program code

Sub Raport()
shell_1 = Shell("excel C:\Users\wrote\Downloads\example.xlsx")
End Sub

\* \* \*

# Path – active workbook

## Result

## Solution

Run program.

## Program code

```
Sub FullName()
MsgBox ActiveWorkbook.FullName
End Sub
```

* * *

# Prompt the user to enter a value

How to prompt the user to enter a value?

## Result

Input box with tile, information and default value.

## Solution

Run program.

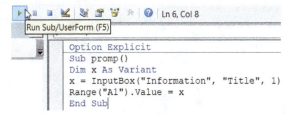

Enter data or accept the default value and click **OK**.

The cell address is stored in the program. The entered value will appear in this cell.

## Program code

```
Option Explicit
Sub promp()
Dim x As Variant
x = InputBox("Information", "Title", 1)
Range("A1").Value = x
End Sub
```

* * *

# Reading – cell value

## Result

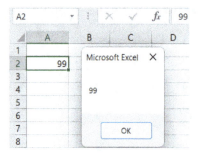

## Screenshots

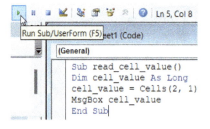

```
Sub read_cell_value()
Dim cell_value As Long
cell_value = Cells(2, 1)
MsgBox cell_value
End Sub
```

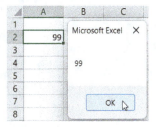

## Program code

```
Sub read_cell_value()
Dim cell_value As Long
cell_value = Cells(2, 1)
MsgBox cell_value
End Sub
```

* * *

# Runing a batch file

In this example first save batch file (see previous chapter)

## Result

## Screenshot

```
Book1 - Sheet1 (Code)
(General)
    Sub Raport()
    b = Shell("C:\Users\wrote\OneDrive\Dokumenty\backup.bat")
    End Sub
```

## Program code

Sub Raport()
b =
Shell("C:\Users\wrote\OneDrive\Dokumenty\backup.bat")
End Sub

# Runing a code

## Solution

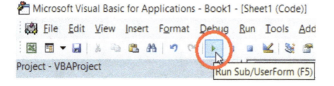

## Keyboard shortcut

F5

* * *

# Runing an application

## Result

For example Calc.

## Screenshot

```
Book1 - Sheet1 (Code)
(General)
    Sub Raport()
    shell_1 = Shell("calc")
    End Sub
```

## Program code

```
Sub Raport()
shell_1 = Shell("calc")
End Sub
```

* * *

# Runing two applications

---

## Result

---

## Screenshot

```
Book1 - Sheet1 (Code)
(General)
    Sub Raport()
    shell_1 = Shell("calc")
    shell_2 = Shell("notepad /")
    End Sub
```

---

## Program code

```
Sub Raport()
shell_1 = Shell("calc")
shell_2 = Shell("notepad /")
End Sub
```

* * *

# Saving worksheet with VBA

## Result

Type: Microsoft Excel Macro-Enabled Worksheet
Authors:
Size: 13.5 KB
Date modified: 3/4/2022 5:25 PM
Availability status: Available on this device

## Screenshot

Follow the number.

4- Location.

5- File name.

6 – File type (important!!!).

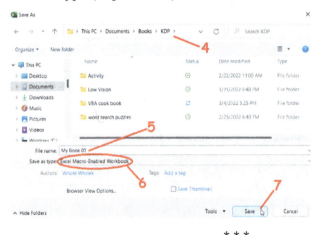

\* \* \*

# Sheet protection

## Result

before

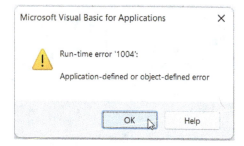

after

## Screenshot

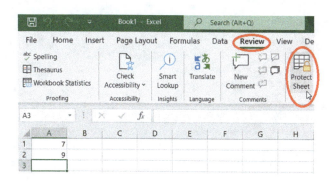

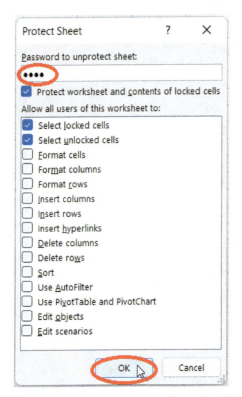

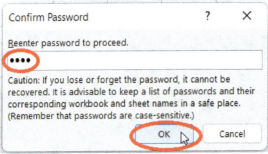

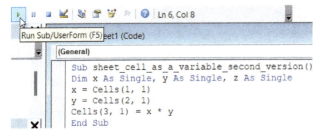

```
Sub sheet_cell_as_a_variable_second_version()
Dim x As Single, y As Single, z As Single
x = Cells(1, 1)
y = Cells(2, 1)
Cells(3, 1) = x * y
End Sub
```

## Program code

```
Sub sheet_cell_as_a_variable_second_version()
Dim x As Single, y As Single, z As Single
x = Cells(1, 1)
y = Cells(2, 1)
Cells(3, 1) = x * y
End Sub
```

* * *

# Text as a variable

## Result

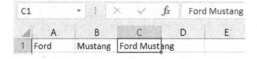

## Screenshot

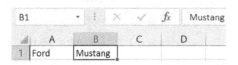

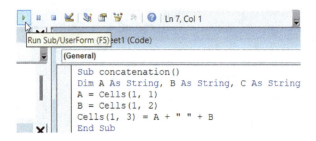

```
Sub concatenation()
Dim A As String, B As String, C As String
A = Cells(1, 1)
B = Cells(1, 2)
Cells(1, 3) = A + " " + B
End Sub
```

## Program code

```
Sub concatenation()
Dim A As String, B As String, C As String
A = Cells(1, 1)
B = Cells(1, 2)
Cells(1, 3) = A + " " + B
End Sub
```

 VBA results cannot be undone by using the Ctrl + Z key combination.

\* \* \*

# The scope of variable declaration

| | |
|---|---|
|  | Attention! If a **Static** expression is used in a variable declaration instead of a **Dim** expression, the variable will retain its value after the procedure completes. The variable will cease to exist, if the procedure ends with an **End** statement. |
|  | If the declaration is placed at the beginning of a module, it covers the entire module in the **Declarations** section. |

# Type mismatch

## Result

## Screenshot

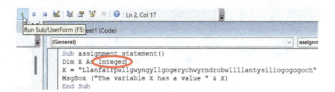

## Program code

Sub assignment_statement()
Dim X As Integer
X =
"Llanfairpwllgwyngyllgogerychwyrndrobwllllantysiliogogog
och"
MsgBox ("The variable X has a value " & X)
End Sub

| | Integer - stores number values that won't take on decimal form. |
|---|---|
| | String - stores text. Can contain numbers, but will store them as a text. |
| | Calculations cannot be performed on numbers stored as a string. |

\* \* \*

# User Form's back color

---

## Result

---

## Screenshot

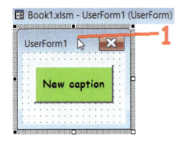

1 – Click this place.

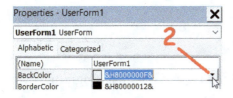

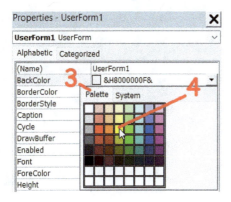

# 6 – To close User Form click **Reset**.

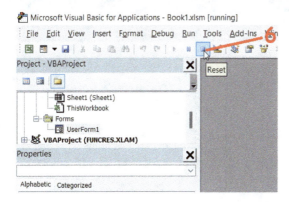

* * *

# Value of variable

This is useful for knowing the value of a variable in a program.

---

## Result

---

## Screenshot

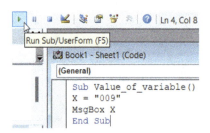

---

## Program code

Sub Value_of_variable()
X = "009"
MsgBox X
End Sub

* * *

# Variables – adding number and number

---

## Result

---

## Screenshot

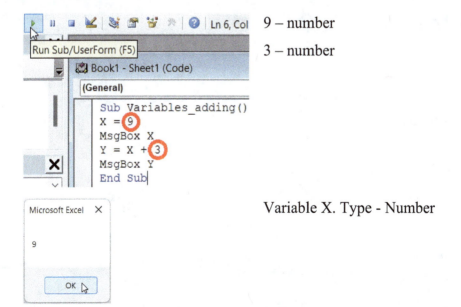

9 – number

3 – number

```
Sub Variables_adding()
X = 9
MsgBox X
Y = X + 3
MsgBox Y
End Sub
```

Variable X. Type - Number

---

Variable Y. It's number too.

## Program code

```
Sub Variables_adding()
X = 9
MsgBox X
Y = X + 3
MsgBox Y
End Sub
```

\* \* \*

# Variables – adding number and text

## Result

# Screenshot

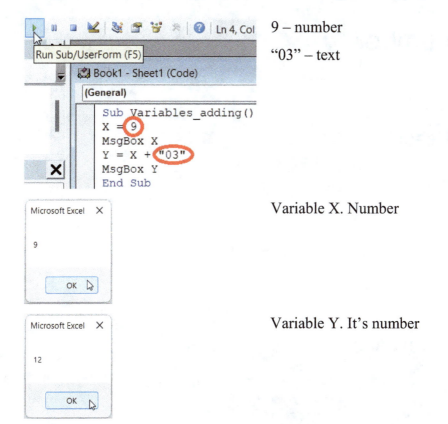

9 – number

"03" – text

Variable X. Number

Variable Y. It's number

# Program code

```
Sub Variables_adding()
X = 9
MsgBox X
Y = X + "03"
MsgBox Y
End Sub
```

* * *

# Variables – adding text and number

---

## Result

---

## Screenshot

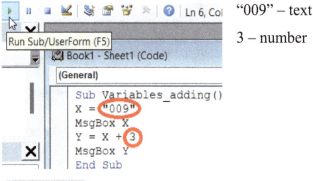

"009" – text

3 – number

Variable X equals 009. Text

Variable Y equals 12. It's number

## Program code

```
Sub Variables_adding()
X = "009"
MsgBox X
Y = X + 3
MsgBox Y
End Sub
```

* * *

# Variables – adding text and text

## Result

# Screenshot

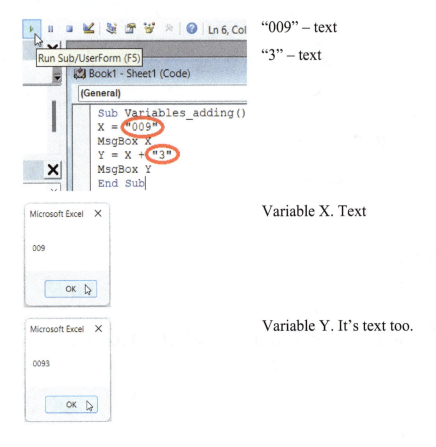

"009" – text

"3" – text

Variable X. Text

Variable Y. It's text too.

# Program code

```
Sub Variables_adding()
X = "009"
MsgBox X
Y = X + "3"
MsgBox Y
End Sub
```

* * *

# Variables - multiplication of text and numbers

## Result

## Screenshot

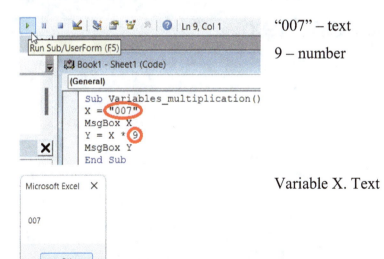

"007" – text

9 – number

Variable X. Text

Variable Y. It's number

## Program code

```
Sub Variables_multiplication()
X = "007"
MsgBox X
Y = X * 9
MsgBox Y
End Sub
```

\* \* \*

# Variables - multiplication of number and text

## Result

# Screenshot

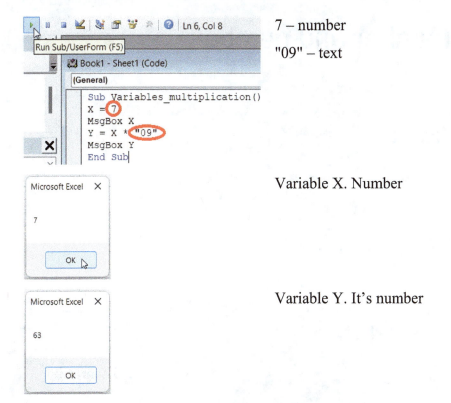

7 – number

"09" – text

Variable X. Number

Variable Y. It's number

# Program code

Sub Variables_multiplication()
X = 7
MsgBox X
Y = X * "09"
MsgBox Y
End Sub

* * *

# Variables - multiplication of number and number

---

## Result

---

## Screenshot

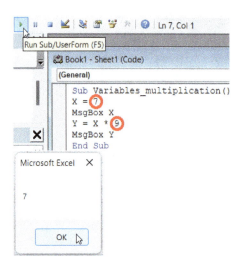

7 – number
9 – number

Variable X.
Number

Variable Y.
Number

## Program code

```
Sub Variables_multiplication()
X = 7
MsgBox X
Y = X * 9
MsgBox Y
End Sub
```

* * *

# Variables - multiplication of text and text

## Result

# Screenshot

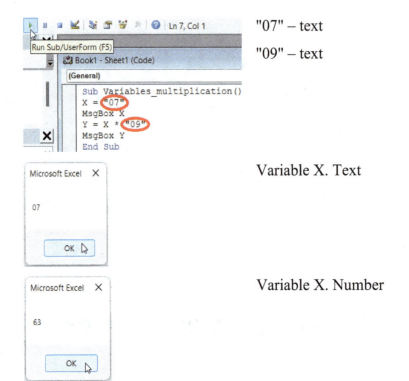

"07" – text

"09" – text

Variable X. Text

Variable X. Number

# Program code

Sub Variables_multiplication()
X = "07"
MsgBox X
Y = X * "09"
MsgBox Y
End Sub

* * *

# Variables – subtracting number and text

## Result

## Screenshot

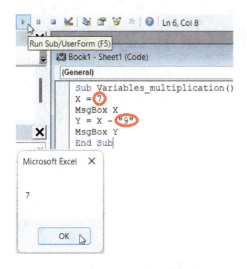

7 – number

"9" – text

Variable X.
Number

Variable Y.
Number

---

## Program code

```
Sub Variables_multiplication()
X = 7
MsgBox X
Y = X - "9"
MsgBox Y
End Sub
```

|  | Attention! The data format was changed without informing the user about it and without asking for confirmation of this operation. |

* * *

# Variables – subtracting text and numbers

---

## Result

# Screenshot

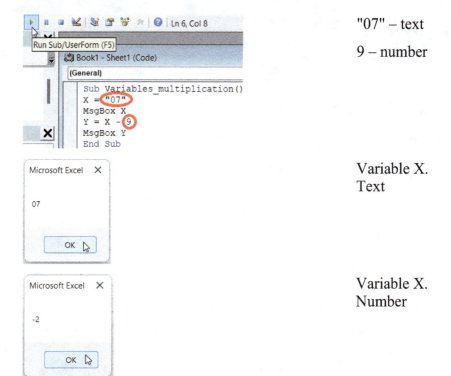

"07" – text

9 – number

Variable X.
Text

Variable X.
Number

# Program code

```
Sub Variables_multiplication()
X = "07"
MsgBox X
Y = X - 9
MsgBox Y
End Sub
```

                    * * *

# Variables – subtracting text and text

## Result

## Screenshot

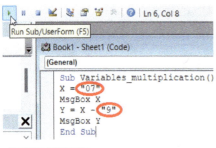

"07" – text

"9" – text

Variable X.
Text

Variable Y.
Number

## Program code

```
Sub Variables_multiplication()
X = "07"
MsgBox X
Y = X - "9"
MsgBox Y
End Sub
```

* * *

# Appendix A. Displaying messages

The MsgBox function enables, among others: displaying the window message, program execution pause until the button is pressed, return of an integer with a value depending on the button pressed.

| Result | Program code |
| --- | --- |

| | Sub message() MsgBox ("Hello world!!!") End Sub |
|---|---|

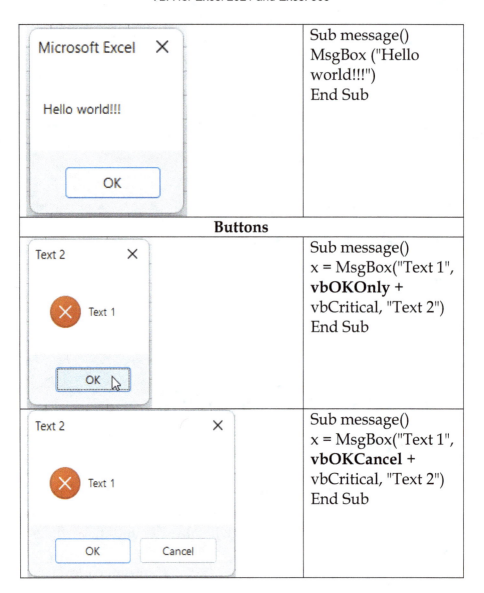

| Buttons | |
|---|---|
| | Sub message() x = MsgBox("Text 1", **vbOKOnly +** vbCritical, "Text 2") End Sub |
| | Sub message() x = MsgBox("Text 1", **vbOKCancel +** vbCritical, "Text 2") End Sub |

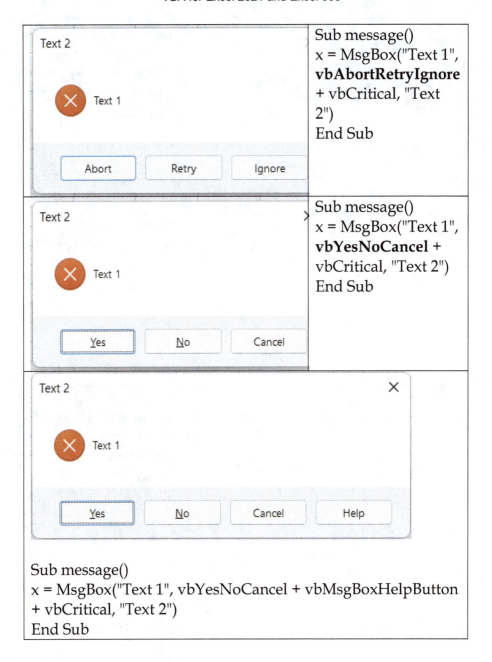

| | |
|---|---|
| Text 2<br><br>❌ Text 1<br><br>[ Abort ] [ Retry ] [ Ignore ] | Sub message()<br>x = MsgBox("Text 1",<br>**vbAbortRetryIgnore**<br>+ vbCritical, "Text<br>2")<br>End Sub |
| Text 2<br><br>❌ Text 1<br><br>[ Yes ] [ No ] [ Cancel ] | Sub message()<br>x = MsgBox("Text 1",<br>**vbYesNoCancel** +<br>vbCritical, "Text 2")<br>End Sub |

Text 2 ❌ Text 1

[ Yes ] [ No ] [ Cancel ] [ Help ]

Sub message()
x = MsgBox("Text 1", vbYesNoCancel + vbMsgBoxHelpButton
+ vbCritical, "Text 2")
End Sub

| | |
|---|---|
| 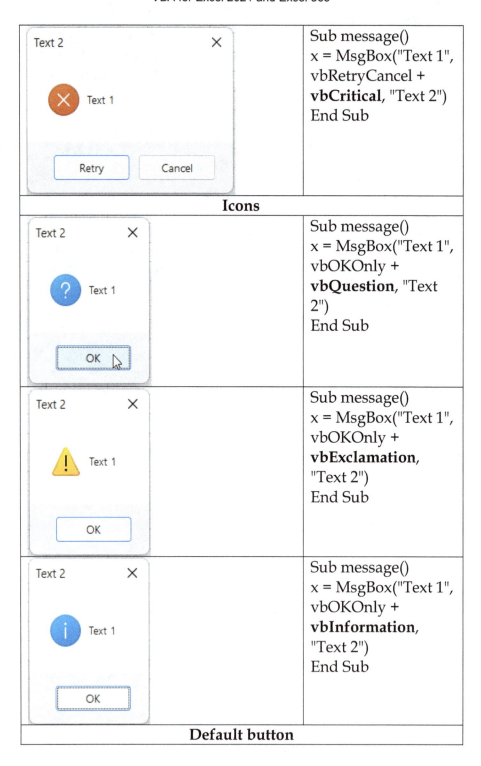 Text 2 ☓ ❌ Text 1 Retry Cancel | Sub message() x = MsgBox("Text 1", vbRetryCancel + **vbCritical**, "Text 2") End Sub |
| **Icons** | |
| Text 2 ☓ ❓ Text 1 OK | Sub message() x = MsgBox("Text 1", vbOKOnly + **vbQuestion**, "Text 2") End Sub |
| Text 2 ☓ ⚠ Text 1 OK | Sub message() x = MsgBox("Text 1", vbOKOnly + **vbExclamation**, "Text 2") End Sub |
| Text 2 ☓ ℹ Text 1 OK | Sub message() x = MsgBox("Text 1", vbOKOnly + **vbInformation**, "Text 2") End Sub |
| **Default button** | |

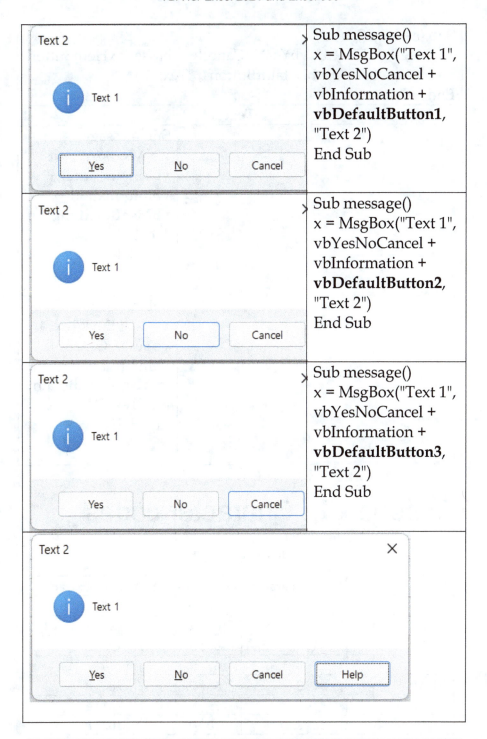

| | Sub message() |
|---|---|
| Text 2 — Text 1 — Yes / No / Cancel | x = MsgBox("Text 1", vbYesNoCancel + vbInformation + **vbDefaultButton1**, "Text 2") End Sub |
| Text 2 — Text 1 — Yes / No / Cancel | Sub message() x = MsgBox("Text 1", vbYesNoCancel + vbInformation + **vbDefaultButton2**, "Text 2") End Sub |
| Text 2 — Text 1 — Yes / No / Cancel | Sub message() x = MsgBox("Text 1", vbYesNoCancel + vbInformation + **vbDefaultButton3**, "Text 2") End Sub |
| Text 2 — Text 1 — Yes / No / Cancel / Help | |

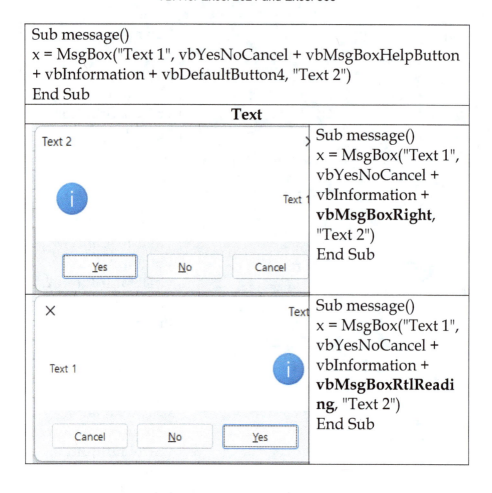

# Appendix B. Character codes

**From 0 to 127**

| Code | Character | Code | Character | Code | Character | Code | Character |
|------|-----------|------|-----------|------|-----------|------|-----------|
| 0 |  | 32 | [space] | 64 | @ | 96 | ` |
| 1 |  | 33 | ! | 65 | A | 97 | a |
| 2 |  | 34 | " | 66 | B | 98 | b |
| 3 |  | 35 | # | 67 | C | 99 | c |
| 4 |  | 36 | $ | 68 | D | 100 | d |
| 5 |  | 37 | % | 69 | E | 101 | e |
| 6 |  | 38 | & | 70 | F | 102 | f |

| | | | | | | | | |
|---|---|---|---|---|---|---|---|---|
| 7 | | 39 | ' | | 71 | G | 103 | g |
| 8 | backspace | 40 | ( | | 72 | H | 104 | h |
| 9 | tab | 41 | ) | | 73 | I | 105 | i |
| 10 | linefeed | 42 | * | | 74 | J | 106 | j |
| 11 | CR | 43 | + | | 75 | K | 107 | k |
| 12 | | 44 | , | | 76 | L | 108 | l |
| 13 | | 45 | - | | 77 | M | 109 | m |
| 14 | | 46 | . | | 78 | N | 110 | n |
| 15 | | 47 | / | | 79 | O | 111 | o |
| 16 | | 48 | | 0 | 80 | P | 112 | p |
| 17 | | 49 | | 1 | 81 | Q | 113 | q |
| 18 | | 50 | | 2 | 82 | R | 114 | r |
| 19 | | 51 | | 3 | 83 | S | 115 | s |
| 20 | | 52 | | 4 | 84 | T | 116 | t |
| 21 | | 53 | | 5 | 85 | U | 117 | u |
| 22 | | 54 | | 6 | 86 | V | 118 | v |
| 23 | | 55 | | 7 | 87 | W | 119 | w |
| 24 | | 56 | | 8 | 88 | X | 120 | x |
| 25 | | 57 | | 9 | 89 | Y | 121 | y |
| 26 | | 58 | : | | 90 | Z | 122 | z |
| 27 | | 59 | ; | | 91 | [ | 123 | { |
| 28 | | 60 | < | | 92 | \ | 124 | | |
| 29 | | 61 | = | | 93 | ] | 125 | } |
| 30 | | 62 | > | | 94 | ^ | 126 | ~ |
| 31 | | 63 | ? | | 95 | _ | 127 | |

CR - carriage return

## From 128 to 255

| Code | Character | Code | Character | Code | Character | Code | Character |
|------|-----------|------|-----------|------|-----------|------|-----------|
| 128 | € | 160 | NBS | 192 | À | 224 | à |
| 129 |  | 161 | ¡ | 193 | Á | 225 | á |
| 130 | , | 162 | ¢ | 194 | Â | 226 | â |
| 131 | ƒ | 163 | £ | 195 | Ã | 227 | ã |
| 132 | „ | 164 | ¤ | 196 | Ä | 228 | ä |
| 133 | … | 165 | ¥ | 197 | Å | 229 | å |
| 134 | † | 166 | ¦ | 198 | Æ | 230 | æ |
| 135 | ‡ | 167 | § | 199 | Ç | 231 | ç |
| 136 | ˆ | 168 | ¨ | 200 | È | 232 | è |
| 137 | ‰ | 169 | © | 201 | É | 233 | é |
| 138 | Š | 170 | ª | 202 | Ê | 234 | ê |
| 139 | ‹ | 171 | « | 203 | Ë | 235 | ë |
| 140 | Œ | 172 | ¬ | 204 | Ì | 236 | ì |
| 141 |  | 173 | SH | 205 | Í | 237 | í |
| 142 | Ž | 174 | ® | 206 | Î | 238 | î |
| 143 |  | 175 | ¯ | 207 | Ï | 239 | ï |
| 144 |  | 176 | ° | 208 | Ð | 240 | ð |
| 145 | ‘ | 177 | ± | 209 | Ñ | 241 | ñ |
| 146 | ’ | 178 | ² | 210 | Ò | 242 | ò |
| 147 | “ | 179 | ³ | 211 | Ó | 243 | ó |
| 148 | ” | 180 | ´ | 212 | Ô | 244 | ô |
| 149 | • | 181 | µ | 213 | Õ | 245 | õ |
| 150 | – | 182 | ¶ | 214 | Ö | 246 | ö |
| 151 | — | 183 | · | 215 | × | 247 | ÷ |
| 152 | ˜ | 184 | ¸ | 216 | Ø | 248 | ø |
| 153 | ™ | 185 | ¹ | 217 | Ù | 249 | ù |
| 154 | š | 186 | º | 218 | Ú | 250 | ú |
| 155 | › | 187 | » | 219 | Û | 251 | û |
| 156 | œ | 188 | ¼ | 220 | Ü | 252 | ü |
| 157 |  | 189 | ½ | 221 | Ý | 253 | ý |
| 158 | ž | 190 | ¾ | 222 | Þ | 254 | þ |
| 159 | Ÿ | 191 | ¿ | 223 | ß | 255 | ÿ |

NBS - no-break space; SH - soft hyphen